Fundamental Ideas of Theosophy

By Bhagwan Das

Copyright © 2021 Lamp of Trismegistus. All rights reserved. No part of this publication may be reproduced or transmitted in any form or by any means, electronic or mechanical, including photocopying, recording, or by any information storage and retrieval system, without permission in writing from Lamp of Trismegistus. Reviewers may quote brief passages.

ISBN: 978-1-63118-571-7

Esoteric Classics

Other Books in this Series and Related Titles

Aurora of the Philosophers by Paracelsus (978-1-63118-507-6)

Clairvoyance and Psychic Abilities by A Besant &c (978-1-63118-403-1)

The Feminine Occult by various authors (978-1-63118-711-7)

Rosicrucian Rules, Secret Signs, Codes and Symbols by various (978-1-63118-488-8)

An Outline of Theosophy by C W Leadbeater (978-1-63118-452-9)

Paracelsus, the Four Elements and Their Spirits by M P Hall (978-1-63118-400-0)

Essays on Ancient Magic by Helena P Blavatsky (978-1-63118-535-9)

Essays on the Esoteric Tradition of Karma by A Besant &c (978-1-63118-426-0)

The Use of Evil by Annie Besant (978-1-63118-532-8)

The Alchemical Catechism of Paracelsus by Paracelsus (978-1-63118-513-7)

Alchemy in the Nineteenth Century by Helena P Blavatsky (978-1-63118-446-8)

Qabbalistic Teachings and the Tree of Life by M P Hall (978-1-63118-482-6)

The Historic, Mythic and Mystic Christ by Annie Besant (978-1-63118-533-5)

The Hidden Mysteries of Christianity by Annie Besant (978-1-63118-534-2)

History, Analysis and Secret Tradition of the Tarot by Hall &c (978-1-63118-445-1)

Crystal Vision Through Crystal Gazing by Frater Achad (978-1-63118-455-0)

The Golden Verses of Pythagoras: Five Translations (978-1-63118-479-6)

Arcane Formulas or Mental Alchemy by W W Atkinson (978-1-63118-459-8)

The Machinery of the Mind by Dion Fortune (978-1-63118-451-2)

The A E Waite Reader: A Selection of Occult Essays (978-1-63118-515-1)

The Leadbeater Reader: A Selection of Occult Essays (978-1-63118-483-3)

Audio versions are also available on Audible, Amazon and Apple

Other Books in this Series and Related Titles

Dreams: What They Are and How They Are Caused (978–1–63118–570–0)

Communication Between Different Worlds by Annie Besant (978–1–63118–569–4)

Animism, Magic and the Omnipotence of Thought by S Freud (978–1–63118–568–7)

Buddhism by F Otto Schrader (978–1–63118–567–0)

Death by W W Westcott (978–1–63118–566–3)

The Religion of Theosophy by Bhagwan Das (978–1–63118–565–6)

The Spirit of Zoroastrianism by Henry S Olcott (978–1–63118–564–9)

The Brotherhood of Religions by Annie Besant (978–1–63118–563–2)

Fourth Book of Maccabees by Josephus (978-1-63118-562-5)

The Story of Ahikar by Ahiqar (978-1-63118-561-8)

Vision of the Spirit by C. Jinarajadasa (978-1-63118-560-1)

Occult Arts by William Q. Judge (978-1-63118-559-5)

Kali the Mother by Sister Nivedita (978-1-63118-558-8)

Love and Death by Sri Aurobindo (978–1–63118–557–1)

Times and Seasons Volume 1, Numbers 4-6 (978-1-63118-556-4)

The Book of John Whitmer by John Whitmer (978-1-63118-554-0)

Interesting Account of Several Remarkable Visions (978-1-63118-553-3)

The Evening and Morning Star Volume 1, Numbers 11 & 12 (978-1-63118-552-6)

Private Diary of Joseph Smith 1832-1834 (978-1-63118-546-5)

An Address to All Believers in Christ Elder David Whitmer (978-1-63118-545-8)

A Manuscript on Far West by Reed Peck (978-1-63118-544-1)

Audio versions are also available on Audible, Amazon and Apple

Table of Contents

Introduction...7

Fundamental Ideas of Theosophy...9

Dawn of Another Renaissance...29

INTRODUCTION

The word "esoteric" can be difficult to define. Esotericism in general can be seen less as a system of beliefs and more as a category, which encompasses numerous, different systems of beliefs. It's a bit of juxtaposition, since the word "esoteric" indicates something that few people know about, while the term itself broadly covers numerous philosophies, practices, areas of study and belief systems.

In a greater sense, Esotericism acts as a storehouse for secret knowledge, which is often considered ancient (by *tradition, if not by fact)*, passed down from generation to generation, in private. At various times in history, simply possessing the knowledge of some of these subjects, was considered illegal and a jailable offence, if discovered. This usually included such general topics as Alchemy, Pharmacology, Qabalah, Hermeticism, Occultism, Ceremonial Magic, Astrology, Divination, Rosicrucianism and so on. Collectively, these areas of study were often referred to as the esoteric sciences.

Sometimes, the outer garment of a subject isn't esoteric, while what is hidden beneath it, is. As an example, Freemasonry isn't necessarily esoteric by nature (at *least not anymore)*, but certain signs, passwords and handshakes given to the candidate during their initiation, are in fact, esoteric, in the sense that they are hidden from the general public.

Today, in the twenty-first century, such topics are readily available at bookstores across the country, and numerous mainsteam publishers offer beginners guides and coffee-table volumes on many of these subjects, intended for mass appeal. Books like *"The Secret"* have turned previously arcane topics into household knowledge. All that being the case, however, it isn't to say that there still aren't buried secrets to uncover, ancient wisdom being ignored and forgotten mysteries to be explored. In fact, it is often that we are only able to further our own studies by standing on the shoulders of these disappearing giants.

Lamp of Trismegistus is doing its part to help preserve humanity's esoteric history by making some of these classics available to those students who are seeking to unearth the knowledge of these ancient colossi.

So, be sure to check other titles from our *Esoteric Classics* series, as well as our *Occult Fiction*, *Theosophical Classics*, *Foundations of Freemasonry Series*, *Supernatural Fiction*, *Paranormal Research Series*, *Studies in Buddhism* and our *Christian Apocrypha Series*. You can also download the audio versions of most of these titles from Amazon, Apple or Audible, for learning on the go.

THE FUNDAMENTAL IDEAS OF THEOSOPHY

By Bhagwan Das

My Dear Brothers and Sisters, if you will suffer me gladly, as the Christian scriptures recommend you to do, then I will venture to say something to you of what seems to me to be the significance of the Resolution that we have passed today.

This is the Foundation Day of the Theosophical Society. It was born in New York thirty-six years ago. It came over to India four years later. Kind fortune, *i.e.,* karma and samskara, led me to enter it twenty- seven years ago. I have some memories, therefore, of its earlier years. And I will, since I have been asked to say something on this occasion, give you my interpretation of the Resolution in the light of that earlier history.

The principle of Universal Brotherhood is referred to in the Resolution both at the beginning and at the end. It is indeed the Alpha and the Omega of Theosophy. It is the soul of the first and foremost object of the T.S. The Masters, who gave to H. P. Blavatsky and H. S. Olcott the three well-known objects of the T.S., and not only one, of course gave them all for a good scientific reason. This I have elsewhere endeavored to indicate [See *The Religion of Theosophy*] — the reason, namely, that they correspond to the three ultimate factors of all consciousness and therefore of all the many religions which Theosophy seeks to harmonize. Yet at various times in the history of the Society, when this fact was somewhat lost sight of, the validity and usefulness of the second and third objects have been disputed. The third especially was at one time almost discarded. But the first has never been disputed. It has always been recognized as the one and the only true guiding star of the Society. And only by honestly endeavoring to keep it steadily in sight have the helmsmen and the oarsmen of the ship of the T.S. been able so far to steer it comparatively safe, through stress and storm. They have not always been able to avoid minor mistakes and consequent shocks and hurts and painful losses. These may be said to have been inevitable in the hurry and bustle and excitement of each difficult time. Yet it may also be said justly that each difficult time was itself the result of the temporary veiling of their eyes from that true star and the turning of them towards some lesser light, some pseudo star; some will-o'-the- wisp of the nature of a mere mortal.

It is good and useful to go back to the origins from time to time for fresh inspiration, for laying in a new store of pure and fresh waters from the springs of life. And this, the Foundation Day of the T.S., is naturally particularly appropriate for the purpose. And I, therefore, on this day invite your attention to the fact that this principle of Universal Brotherhood, the recognition of which all the workers of the Society, prominent or unprominent, each in his own way and degree, are seeking to secure from the various peoples of the earth — this principle is an Impersonal Principle, and not a personal fact.

As soon as we ask ourselves what is the source, the basis, the support of Universal Brotherhood, so soon do we find ourselves driven perforce to something, which is not a person, to Something which includes all persons, high and low, great and small, brilliant and commonplace.

Each one of us may believe, nay, probably, must believe, in some one or other person or personage, as more helpful to his soul and body than any other. But every one of us cannot but believe *more* in this Impersonal Principle, if he is consciously sincere and consistent member of the Society of which the first object is the spread of the recognition of Universal Brotherhood.

Any one of us may reject, nay, probably, must reject, some particular person or some particular opinion. But this Impersonal Principle, which lies behind Universal Brotherhood and alone justifies recognition of it, he cannot but believe in, however dimly, howbeit sub-consciously. He cannot reject it consciously and yet remain really and deliberately a member of the T.S. Obviously, this is true only of Universal Brotherhood — not of any lesser, any restricted, limited, separatist brotherhoods. The source of such — and the world is full of them — is of course a person, always; the emphasizing of a person and the deriving of life and activity solely from him is the time-old and natural method of separating and establishing a restricted and exclusive family out of Universal Brotherhood, and this method may well be followed by any one to whom such a result seems desirable. Polarization round centers is the recognized method of the *cleavage* of cells. But the source and the support of Universal Brotherhood can only be something which is Universal, not personal. Diffusion and pervasion of the vital fluid of the Universal Religion of Impersonal or All-personal Atman to the outmost periphery of the human race, is the way of its true growth as an ever-more-completely-united whole.

Because of the Impersonality and therefore all-inclusiveness of this its nourishing and supporting Principle, has it been found possible at all to carry the T.S. without entire destruction through disputes such as have completely wrecked other bodies not guided by the same guide. In this Impersonal Principle, and in it alone, is the seed of all reconciliation and permanent tolerance and harmony and unification.

In personalities, on the other hand, in shibboleths and rallying-cries and the excessive pushing forward of personal names, there has always thriven through all time past, and will continue to flourish through all time to come, the seed of challenge and counter-challenge, of division and dispute and strife between man and brother-man, the seed of dissensions and suspicions and criminations and recriminations, of charges and counter-charges of adulation and traducement, of blind worship and mad criticism, of disloyalty to truth and disloyalty to person. In the past history of the T.S., whenever there has been a 'shaking' of the very foundations of the T.S. which has been left behind sad cracks and gaps in the superstructure, it has *always* been due to an exaggeration of the person above the Impersonal Principle. Religious wars have ever been wars for personal names. I am not aware of any war for the Impersonal. The followers of the cult of the Impersonal have been plentifully called tiresome bores, imbeciles, talkers of unmeaning words, lifeless dullards — but they have never provoked wars and battles so far as I have heard. But of course I may be mistaken. None can say they have compassed all history, and I can say it least of all. Yet this is undoubted that there has been much bloodshed in the *names* of the Christ, the Prophet, even the Buddha and the Jina, to say nothing of smaller names.

Because of this, I humbly think, the ship of Theosophy — Atma-vidya, Brahma-vidya, the Science of the Self, the Science of the Eternal and Infinite, as ever diligently explained by H. P. Blavatsky and H. S. Olcott — was launched upon the troubled waters of modern civilization, when that civilization had grown to be able to supply to that ship the steam-power which alone could enable it to circumnavigate the earth; and it was launched without a proper name, but with only a general and descriptive one, to slowly usher in the epoch of buddhi and humanism and Universal Brotherhood, and bid a gradual farewell to the epoch of manas and individualism and separatist religious names and forms.

Material science, working by stream and rail and wire and the printing press, has over-shot its mark of individualism and linked up the countries and religions of the world — though the linking up is painful and discordant because of the wrong spirit pervading it — and has thus made the world-wide spread of the message of Universal Brotherhood, which is the essence of Theosophy, not only necessary but also possible and almost easy too. Without it such spread would be obviously impossible. It remains for the T.S. by remaining true to that message, to return the unconscious and unwilling kindness of material science consciously, by spiritualizing that science and helping to spread it broadcast in beneficial and not harmful forms; by converting the linking chains — at present of hard iron — that bind together the races of men, into ornaments of soft gold worn eagerly by each to please the eyes of all the others. And the only alchemy that can change the iron of the age into gold is the replacement more and more of the person by the Impersonal. This also is the only alchemy, which can solve effectively in each individual case those endless doubts and soul-tortures, 'Am I losing my soul or am I being saved?' 'Am I in the clutches of the Devil, or am I in the embrace of the Christ?' 'Am I being subtly led to Avichi by those of the Left Hand, or gently guided to Nirvana by those of the Right Hand?' All these disappear finally, when, and only when, we fix our gaze upon the Impersonal.

I would therefore reiterate what I said before, that while every member of the T.S. may very well believe in any given person, he ought to believe more in That which is beyond all persons, And this is indeed the world-old teaching that has been given by all the recognized great Teachers of the past, and presumably will be given by all the Teachers of the future. None has asked his followers to worship him beyond the Atman. All have asked their followers to seek for the Atman within each. But the followers have often shamed their leaders and often led those leaders (or their names) and themselves into dissensions, ever unconsciously mistaking the subtle self-displaying wish to *appear devoted* to the teacher for the wish *to devote themselves to the cause* advocated by the teacher. The *Avadana-kalpa-lata* of Kshemendra, a Buddhist work, tells of a great fight between a band of Shramanas, followers of the Buddha, and a band of Kshapanas, followers of the Jina, during the very lifetime of those two great Teachers, each a strenuous preacher of uttermost harmlessness and peace!

One of the precious books of Theosophy, a veritable little scripture in its way, *Light on the Path*, fallen somewhat into neglect, perhaps, latterly, says: "Nothing that is embodied, nothing that is conscious of separation, nothing that is out of the Eternal, can aid you"; and obviously the Eternal is the Impersonal. To multiply quotations from the ancient writings to the same effect would be an endless task.

It is plain that there have been many teachers in the past, indeed countless, so some of the scriptures say, and there will be as many in the future. But the Teaching has ever been and must ever be one and the same: "Seek the Atman", "Find the Atman", "Know Thyself". That is the End. These, the teachers, are the means; the means to wipe away the dust of degenerate ages which settles down upon, and hides from time to time, the glory of that eternal self-same Teaching; the means to put more vitality into the dimmed eyes of men that cannot clearly see the Infinite Light; indispensably necessary means to progress, worthy of all honor and reverence, in their respective degrees, — but in no case to supersede that Final Goal, which should never be lost of. To shut it out of sight consciously, after having gained even the faintest and most purely intellectual glimpse of it — this is the only and the greatest possible disloyalty to any genuine teacher of Atma-Vidya. If this disloyalty is avoided, all other minor loyalties are sure to be fulfilled in most due measure. Not to have seen that Final Goal yet, may be quite natural and even proper, for those not yet ready to enter the T.S., the younger brothers, as they have been called. For such there are many preparatory associations, orders, leagues, by working in which, perhaps, they may soon attain the needed majority that is required by the rules of the T.S., literally and metaphorically. But for those that are in the T.S. to forget it, for them to place the person above the Impersonal — were to endanger the well-being of the whole Society, were to throw doubt upon the whole world-wide movement now in progress, under many names and not only one, for unity and federation and co-operation in all departments of human life. On the other hand, to honor the person as below and after the Impersonal — nay, not only one person but many persons, each reverencing his own elder most but ever assiduously bearing in mind that other elders rightly claim the reverence of others — this is a source of much health and strength and inspiration to good work, for the young and the old alike.

The *Bhagavad-Gita* (Chapter XII) tells us that the easier preliminary ways, of leaning on another, are to be placed only before those who are not yet capable of taking up the harder tasks; and that more difficult work should be expected from the older and stronger, the work of standing on their own feet.

Indeed, it may well be said that the elder brothers perform their duty loyally to their trust only when, in leading on the younger brothers up the steps of the ladder, they miss no occasion, indeed diligently take every occasion, to bring home to the minds of the youngers, that the ladder is only the means to reaching the top of the tower and not to be made a dwelling-place, that the person is only a means to the Impersonal and any one individual only a guide to the Universal Atman. Also we have to remember that this present and latest advent of Theosophy is by way of reaction against and correction of the great growth of scientific materialism. And he who would enter into Theosophy through the Theosophical Society, may safely be presumed to have recapitulated in his own individual mind the movement of thought in the racial mind and to have become able to think critically about scientific materialism; and that implies readiness to think About the Impersonal, albeit dimly at first. To believe in a person more than in the Impersonal, *after* this stage, is indeed to stunt the growth of the soul; for that *growth* is undisputedly from other-reliance to Self-reliance.

To every earnest soul there comes, by a psycho-physical law, generally in the third septenate of the years of its bodily envelope, *i.e.,* between the fourteenth and the twenty-first years, a yearning to understand the meaning of life and death, joy and sorrow, virtue and sin, to understand the origin and end of all the infinite movement around.

This is the age of the soul's adolescence, in the body as well as in the spirit. In this difficult time, the soul has to adjust itself anew toward the material envelope as well as towards the Higher Self. It recapitulates in this important septenate, the racial experience of the third Root-Race. Shall it run wholly matter-wards — like the bears and the monkeys of the *Ramayana?* Shall it run wholly spirit-wards

— like the Haryashvas and the Shabalashvas of the *Bhagavata?* High exaltations, deep depressions, ecstasies of joy, agonies of despair, wild romance, fairy imagination, chivalry, knight-errantry, gross blunders, noble dreams — all is summed up in the one word: youth! And underneath all runs the current of a deep melancholy, the sadness that is inseparable from spring — is life worth living, is all the trouble worth while? Religious conversions, and alas! even more often, *per-versions;* noble ambitions and resolutions, and, more often, vicious degenerations and sex-crimes, at our present stage of evolution and in the existing conditions of life — are most observable at this period of life. The call of the flesh is one the soul; and, by necessary undercurrent of re-action, the call of the spirit also. The glamour and bloom of youth and of the senses, in one's own body and in the bodies of others, attract irresistibly; the Eternal Consciousness recognizes the inevitable ending in dust and ashes. And the soul rushes frenziedly, now towards the upper pole of the human magnet — renunciation, wisdom, the knowledge and love of the All; now towards the lower pole — selfish pursuit, cleverness, the love of the lower, smaller, self and sex, ahankara. he elders of our race, the Manus, Rshis and Prajapatis, have found and prescribed sweet reconciliation (only the best possible in the circumstances) for spirit and matter, for upward striving and downward drag, in holy wedlock and in the joyous pain of daily sacrifice for family and friends and dependents, the daily five yajnas — whereby the wheel of Brahman is kept turning. But in order that the reconciliation be effected in the fullest and most perfect measure possible, it is indispensable that that travail, the war in Hamlet's young soul — typical of all young souls — of to be or not to be — be allayed; that all doubts and questions be solved satisfactorily.

And the very first question that such a soul puts to itself is: "What is the final cause and meaning of all this meaningless, causeless, ruthless turmoil and tyranny that we call the Universe". This is the first question to be asked and also the last to be answered. But it can be answered only if the seed of the yearning is carefully tended and nursed to bud and blossom and fruit. If the counselor sought by the yearner tells him, on the other hand, thoughtlessly: "Be more modest, try to understand only what is within your reach, you are too young, take a personal guru to worship, obey unreasoningly and follow, etc.", then indeed he does a grievous wrong, although unconsciously; he deprives the earnest soul of its birth-right, he misleads it away to a false contentment with the mess of pottage, makes it lose its chance for this life, gives it only the finite when it might have had the Infinite.

After the third septenate of years, as Manu says, the chances of gaining the inner vision of the Universal are very small.

Small worldly ambitions, the mastering of minor departments of knowledge, the gaining of passing objects — require so much time, concentration and effort. Can the secret of the Universe, the secret of immortality — and immortality is the unshakeable *conviction* of immortality, the *realization* of it as the inalienable right of the Spirit in every living thing—can this be gained by dilettante dawdling, or by playing with mortal idols, or even by whole-hearted worship of that which is palpably not immortal? The principle of infinity lies hid in every self-reproducing seed and germ of life. The glamour and romance of youth, the fairy moonlight with which all its surroundings are washed and painted — have all come *from within itself;* youth itself has put these upon others and then fallen down in prostrate worship before them. They are the faint reflections and shadows of this principle of infinity — Brahman — beginning to stir within itself, which it credits away to others. At the human stage, more and more, this principle tends to turn upon itself rather than outwards upon the lesser things of name and form. And then appears that supreme and virgin passioning of the soul, called vairagya, which is the necessary condition of the espousal of the small self by the Great Self. As the *Upanishats* say, the Atman unveils itself only to the soul, which It Itself espouseth, and none is so espoused which yearns not strongly, whole-heartedly, with undivided power of passion, for that great consummation. The soul, which fritters itself away in smaller interests; which spends the 'infinite' power within it, in the painting with glamour and beauty bloom, and the enveloping with its best love and reverence of lesser objects, personal idols and ideals, however subtly poetized and refined and elevated; the soul which directs not its concentrated longing towards the Infinite, hiding within itself — that soul loses its chance for this life — of course there are other lives.

It is not quite well, yet it is not quite ill, if the glorious romance of youth leads into sanctified marriage of the household life — which is the most important and most honored of all lives, plane after plane — *without* having first secured the Infinite. It is not ill, because it means only that the soul is not quite ready for the Infinite yet. But it is ill, it is very sad indeed, if that romantic search should lead to neither, but to hollow imitations thereof. Theosophy, more essentially than charity, which is only one of its fruits, begins at home. The Theosophy, which leads to no home, which helps no home, which breaks up any home, is not Theosophy, but something masquerading in the stolen garb of Theosophy. Virtues and good qualities should be educed and cultivated for their own sake, or for the sake of the living fathers and mothers and brothers and sisters and spouses and natural relations and friends — at least as much as for any comparative outsider. At least such is the teaching of Manu. And in this reference may be considered the dangers of the premature arousing of a highly emotional and *exalte* condition in the young with regard to persons outside of the natural home. It is likely to interfere with their due intellectual growth and to produce other most unfortunate consequences besides — consequences well-known to all students and observers of the past and current history of personal religions and sects. For a high surge of even devotional emotion, if not kept steadily directed upwards, by matured knowledge, experience and wisdom, irresistibly runs downwards to the lower pole of the human magnet and breeds the most unhappy sex-degenerations.

But if the original yearning for the Infinite is carefully fostered and guided and the Impersonal ever kept before the eyes of the aspirant — the *Bhagavad-Gita* is a manual of the Impersonal and is studied by so many of our members — then indeed the seed will proceed to its natural blooming and fruiting first, in the intellectual vision of the Infinite and Impersonal, then in Its fuller ethical assimilation, and finally in Its greater and greater practical realization.

And this thought gives us some clue to periodical differences in the *methods* of the Teaching, while its *substance* remains unchanged. Two thousand years ago, Jesus Christ is reported to have cried: "Suffer the little children to come unto Me". Today, Atma-Vidya, which is the Teacher of all teachers has directed them to cry through the Theosophical Society". Induce the *grown-ups* to gather round Me; and induce them by means of these three objects of the T.S., wherein is the seed of all religions and of Universal Religion, the seed of (1) all Ethics; (2) all Knowledge; (3) all Yoga-powers; by means of the deliberate cultivation of Universal Brotherhood, the study of the origins and innermost truths common to all religions, the deliberate investigation of the powers latent in the being, the Self, the Atman of each which is, indeed, the Atman, of all".

It has been thought by some members now and then that a more *precise* set of beliefs, in the nature of a person-cult, is likely to be more suitable and effective. It no doubt might be so, for some minds and for any special purposes those members may have in view. But so far as the Theosophical ideal is concerned, I humbly believe that the very amorphousness of the objects of the T.S. is the guarantee of its vital elasticity and growth, and that a precise definition into a cut-and-dry *credo* would mean its ossification and death. For I conceive the mission of the T.S. to be not to usher in a *new* personal religion, but (1) to harmonize, (2) to rationalize, and (3) to broaden the *existing* religions by means of the pursuit of its three objects respectively, and gradually to enable them, of their own free-will and intelligent consent, to merge into the Eternal Universal Religion, in the persons of the most advanced of each religion first, and then of the less advanced by means of those.

If these three obviously impersonal, yet unquestionable and indefeasible objects are steadily pursued in the right spirit (and the General and Sectional councils and office-bearers should make it their duty to carefully think out the ways and means of such steady pursuit), then surely the personal and formal elements — which, and which alone, are the separative and discord-breeding factors in any given religion — will be gradually subordinated into their proper place; then the common Soul portions, the essential principles, of all the living religions will be enabled to coalesce into one Scientific Religion of spirit-matter; and then will all the special religions and families of mankind merge into one great family inspired by Atma-Vidya or Theosophy, the three parts or thirds of which are (a) a Universal Love and Brotherliness and tolerant Helpfulness towards all, (b) a Universal Metaphysic of the Laws of Consciousness, and (c) a Universal Practical Science of the transformations of matter under the stress of that Consciousness, *i.e.,* Yoga-Shastra proper, superphysical Science, or 'Occultism' as it is currently called for want of a better word.

If these views are at all just, it follows that any over-accentuation of a person, within the T.S., is very likely to sin against the first object, even though unwittingly. One of the most important practical benefits of the membership of the T.S. is that it brings a person into contact with the followers of other creeds on terms not only of mutual tolerance but of respect and sympathy for the faiths of each other. And as each member necessarily has relations and friends outside the T.S., this tolerance and respect and sympathy for different faiths gradually spread from him to these others; and so in a small and slow and quiet but sure way is helped on the work of bringing about peace and good-will between the different religions. But the prime condition of success along these lines is that every member should carefully avoid all excess, all vehemence, all emotional violence, in the pushing of his own views, especially as regards the spiritual and religious super-eminence of any persons, and yet more emphatically of persons still in the flesh. Each and every member of the T.S. has, no doubt, a perfect right to his views and, it would seem, to advocate them also, but this should be done in a mild way and only so far as he can do so without hurting the feelings of any other brother within the T.S. As to where reasonable advocacy ends and fanaticism begins, where mutual benefit by exchange of knowledge ends and mutual harm by self- assertion begins — that cannot be laid down in precise words and must be left to the tact, good sense, and observation of the actual effects on each other's feelings, of the members concerned. But one thing is fairly clear—any very impassioned advocacy of any particular view and especially of any *person-cult* is very likely to tread on the toes of others by the inevitable implication and challenge that other persons honored by others are not deserving of the same honor as one's own ideal. Too loud and proof-less assertion of the overwhelming merits of any one individual, unavoidably, by a psychological law, provokes comparisons; and comparisons are ever proverbially 'odious,' 'invidious,' pregnant with evil consequences. And hence all such excessive advocacy is likely to retard the work of establishing peace and goodwill amongst the various living religions.

Holding such views, it seems to me natural to invite your attention repeatedly to the significance of the first object of the T.S. to which we have all subscribed, and which we have referred to in the Resolution passed today. So far, the leaders of the T.S. have whole-heartedly subscribed to this significance. Our present beloved President has ever made it her proud and noble claim that through many mistakes and wanderings she has ever been a follower of the beacon-light of Truth as something irrespective of persons. She has recommended that same attitude to all her hearers and readers, and she has told us that the last and the deepest Truth that she has succeeded in finding is the Truth embodied in Theosophy and the T.S. with their first and foremost object of Universal Brotherhood based on the implied Impersonal Principle of the Universal Atman. And I feel that we do right to express our loyal adherence to that Principle, in sending our greetings by this Resolution, today, to her as the successor of H. P. Blavatsky and H. S. Olcott The early history of the T.S., the earlier bands of its workers who bore the brunt of its vicissitudes when times were far harder for it than they are now, even those two principal names of H. P. Blavatsky and H. S. Olcott are now naturally becoming somewhat obscure to the vision of the new generation of members, amidst the rush and pressure of current affairs. But we know from history that a present, which forgets the past will itself be short-lived in the memory of the future. And we do right today, therefore, in our Resolution especially to remember H. S. Olcott the story of whose great lecturing tours in India with their accompaniment of magnetic healing of the halt, the maimed, the paralyzed and the blind will read some day like a chapter from the Bible; and to remember H.P.B. whose physical and superphysical siddhis were proved, as none others have been proved since, to the most confirmed, habitual and lifelong scoffers and skeptics, converting them into famous workers for the T.S., and whose stores of occult knowledge, as embodied in *The Secret Doctrine* — many portions of which, we are informed, are the direct work of various Masters themselves — continue to form the inexhaustible pabulum of subsequent workers.

Such are the few thoughts that occur to me on this, the Foundation Day of the T.S. It seems to me that the highest loyalty and devotion we can show to the Founders of the T.S. is devotion and loyalty to the Principle to which they were devoted and loyal, the Impersonal Principle which underlies that Universal Brotherhood for the recognition of which they worked their life long.

And, indeed, is it or is it not true that Atma-Vidya, God-Wisdom, Theosophy, is the *End;* and all possible teachers of it, of the past, the present, and the future, but the *means* to it? And if it is so, then should not all of us, and even more especially the office-bearers of the T.S. take unceasing care that we do not, wittingly or un-wittingly, help to make the End the means, and the means the End?

All the scriptures of all the nations of all times and all climes repeat the one teaching 'Seek and find the God *within*'. 'None else compels', 'Within yourselves deliverance must be found', 'None other than Thou can help Thee', 'Thou art that', 'The Kingdom of Heaven is within you'.

Uplift the Atman by the Atman and degrade it not; the self is the only enemy of the Self, and the Self its only real brother, helper, friend. *Bhagavad-Gita* (vi—5)

The lost religions of Assyria, Chaldaea, Egypt, Mexico, Peru said it. The living religions of the Manu, the Zoroaster, the Buddha, the Jina, the Acharya Shankara, the Christ, the Prophet say it. The sages and philosophers from Socrates to Fichte, Hegel and Schopenhauer, but ring changes on the same. In India, the latest great teachers of both Hindu and Muslim have nothing else to say. We may perhaps quote from some of these, not so well-known as the scriptures amongst the learned, yet verily standing for the scriptures to the unlearned in India.

The much studied Saadi says:

He was not lost who turned his face away From worldliness—he found Him-Self that day.

Kabir sings with his own matchless earnestness and pathos:

O my soul! beloved bond-slave!
Where and wherefore seekest thou for Me!
Am I not evermore most near to thee?
Not in or of thine own flesh, bone or blood,
Or any others' flesh or blood am I
But in and of the very Faith of Self, Thy-Self am I!

And Shah Bulla, the famous Musalman faqir and sage and teacher of the Panjab, repeats it to the setting of gentle yet most pithy and epigrammatic humour:

> *But do just try to seek the Seeker, Friend!*
> *Too long hast thou sought Him in Other-homes!*
> *It is just possible Thy-Self mightst be*
> *The One Beloved Friend of all the world,*
> *Whom thou art chasing madly through the woods!*

And Nanak, the first Guru of the Sikks, assures us:

> *Nanak reiterateth evermore —*
> *Not till the soul shall recognize It-Self, Shall it the mire of errors wash away!*

It seems to me therefore, and I humbly submit it for the careful consideration of the members and all the office-bearers of the T.S., that all other activities and pursuits of special person-cults should be regarded as only secondary outlets for superfluous energy, and that it is our primary duty to push the work of revitalizing within the heart of each living religion the *common truths* of Theosophy by means of the systematic pursuit of the three objects of the T.S., and thereby help on the divine plan of the spontaneous fusing of all those hearts into one.

At least so it seems to me. But this may be a constitutional defect of mine, forever since I can remember, the Impersonal has ever been to me more than the person. And I have therefore, at the outset begged of you to suffer me gladly for a while. And because you have suffered me gladly thus far, therefore I am emboldened to repeat yet once more:

Believe in the person, some person, many pre-sons, as your inclinations lead, but believe *more* in the Impersonal. Be devoted to, revere, nay worship, a person, some person, many persons — for, without such, life loses its savor and sweetness; but be *more* devoted to, revere *more,* worship *more,* the Impersonal — for, without such, life loses its foundations, loses itself, perishes in a riot of discord. And adapting the words of the English poet to my purpose, I will say in conclusion:

> *Atman! the Universal Soul of all —*
> *To Whom our self-deluded mind, that takes*
> *Full easily all impressions from below,*
> *Will not look up, or half-contemns the height*
> *To which it won't, fancying it cannot, climb, Thinking it could not*
> *breathe in that fine air, That pure severity of perfect light,*
> *Yearning for warmth and color which it finds*
> *In lesser selves, reflections of itself —*
> *O ! let us lead this self-deluded mind*
> *Of ours, from this darkness to That Light,*
> *From passing phantom forms unto the Truth, From mortal clingings*
> *unto the Immortal,*
> *And see That Highest and most Human too, Which is the One Solo*
> *Found of Life and Love. It is our duty e'er to love the Highest,*
> *It surely were our profit did we know,*
> *It were our deepest pleasure did we see,*
> *We needs must love the Highest most when we Behold It—loving all*
> *else lesser, less.*

THE DAWN OF ANOTHER RENAISSANCE

by Bhagavan Das

The Great New Movements of the Oversoul

GREAT waves of thought, of emotion, of action, most notably of thought, have been surging for the last fifty years, in the Oversoul of Humanity. They are of a somewhat new kind, such as are scarcely to be met with in the past, as recorded in what is recognised as "history by the modern mind. In Samskrt they call that Oversoul by the name of Sutr-ātmā, literally the "Thread-Soul". The Arabic names are Ruh-ul- Alam,-Ruh-ul-Qaum. Mass-mind, Mahat-Buddhi, Collective-Intelligence, Samashti-Buddhi, or even plain Public-Opinion, Loka-mata, are other recognised aspects and well-known names, Samskrt and English, of that same Thing. It is that *Esprit de corps*, that "public *Spirit*", which "threads", individuals together and makes it possible for them to speak in terms of the unitive and inclusive "We" instead of the separatist and exclusive "I". It is the principle of fellow-feeling, of sympathy; the principle which makes fellow-feeling and sympathy possible; for God is Love, in a very practical psychological sense. It has a curious knack of, and a unique faculty for, contracting into the narrowest familism and expanding into the widest humanitarianism, "smaller than the smallest, greater than the greatest", as the *Upanishats* say. It ranges from just above sheer pure egoism (if such a thing is possible, which it is not) to the most extensive altruism, passing through many kinds and degrees of clan, tribe, group, horde, sect, creed, class, caste, profession, sub-race, nation, race, sex, etc.. In current symbols of ideas, Socialism stands for the We- feeling, Individualism for the I-feeling. There is radical and perpetual antagonism between the two. Yet, also, both are necessary, inevitable, always inseparable. Abolish one wholly; the other will also disappear at once, automatically.

Sleep, *pralaya*, will be the result, wherein alone there is absolute equality, homogeneity, indeed identity, absence of all difference. The two are as the connected and continuous halves of a see-saw. Lower one end, the other is raised. Cut away one, the other falls down too. The universe is made up of such "pairs of opposites" in every department, in all aspects.

Synthesis of Inseparable Opposites

The problem before us is: Shall the individualistic-I-spirit be allowed to continue to prevail, in and by blind, frantic, wasteful competition, or shall a fair preponderance be given to the socialistic-We- spirit and co-operation reign throughout mankind as in a joint family ? Which side of the ethico-spiritual human see-saw shall be kept higher and which lower ?

Conscious Intellect and Individualism

The newness of the psycho-physical waves, above referred to, consists in this that they are attacking this problem more and more consciously, purposefully, deliberately, as perhaps was never before done in history; and that they are tending to raise the socialistic end of the see-saw higher. As is said in "theosophical" literature, in the very long evolution of the Human Race, developing faculty after faculty, stage by stage, it is the special work of the "fifth Sub-Race", *i.e.*, the European, broadly speaking, of the "fifth Race", *i.e.*, the Âryan, to develop self-conscious Intellect, the egoistic individualistic "fifth principle". The "modern" mind is therefore putting into terms of wakeful deliberate intellect, what was formerly experienced by the race with lesser conscious clearness, in the shape of emotion-instinct-intuition, with the intelligence half awake and half asleep, so to say, *feeling* rather than *perceiving*. We find the process recapitulated today, more or less definitely, in each individual life, growing through childhood and adolescence into maturity. Thus it comes about that the modern mind is discussing economical, political, social, and even psychological and religious problems (to say nothing of those of physical science) with a. wealth of minute detail of facts and figures, statistics and arguments, and almost overwhelmingly vast collections of information about almost all the countries of the earth, as was never done, or, at any rate, has not been found yet, in any previous historical period. And, be it noted, the strengthening of "individuality", *i.e.*, of the psychical sense of separate personality (as distinguished from the earlier tribal "group"-feeling), and the intensification of "individualism", *i.e.*, of individualistic competition, of ego-istic self-ish struggle, are the natural consequences and concomitants of this phase of human evolution, *viz.*, the development of self-conscious intellect; also that, after sufficient experience of this phase, the tendency is natural, too, to a reaction, and a reversion to the "group" feeling, on a higher level, with richer contents of conscious intelligence, in the shape of Socialism.

The Reign of Individualism

Now, whatever may have happened in prehistoric, legendary, "ancient" *purãnic* times, such history as the modern mind believes in, seems — but the present writer's reading therein is very limited, it must be confessed — to present continuously the picture of the thought, feeling, and activity of the Individualistic spirit predominant.

In Religion, human beings have, so long, mostly preferred to believe in an extra-cosmical, personal, individual, almighty Creator, sitting in heaven and doing with his creatures what he wills; and in his vicegerent, sitting on the earth, the chief 'priest', 'wizard', 'magician', 'medicine-man', 'wise man' of the tribe or nation or race, as the case may be, the super-Brãhmana, Jagad-Guru, Lama, Pope, Khalîfa, etc., the theocrat, in brief. In Politics, the great conqueror and wholesale butcher, the emperor, the *shāhan- shāh*, the *sāmrāt*, *chakravartī*, *sārvabhauma*, the super-Kshattriya, the autocrat (of whom the aristocrat and bureaucrat may be regarded as sub-varieties), has been given praise and glory and homage by mankind generally and historians specially. In Economics, the billionaire, the railway-king, the cotton- king, the wheat-king, the oil-king, and now the automobile-emperor, the super-Vaishya, the plutocrat, has been the subject of well-nigh universal admiration and envy. Mention must not be omitted here, of the "party-boss", master of "tammany" and "graft" and "boodle". who is reported to create and demolish presidents of republics and prime ministers of constitutional monarchies, by strokes of his pen on the leaves of his cheque-book; who can bring about wars between nations or stop them, at will, by giving or withdrawing financial help, just as may suit the business interests of Capital; who can reduce military valour and scientific knowledge (*Kshattriya* and *Brāhmana*), both, to the condition of purchased slaves, to further the purposes of that Capital, and prostitute what should be the holy defenders and promoters of human happiness, for the ruin of millions of homes in all countries, and who thereby firmly binds together "politics" and "economics", and newly justifies the earlier appellation of the "new" science, *viz.*, "political economy". In War, until very recently, in East and West alike, the personal prowess of the commander of the army has been the main deciding factor, and a stray shaft or shot striking him down, has often sufficed to convert a victory into defeat; If an arrow had not found the eye of Harold at Senlac, the Norman would not have trampled down the Saxon in England. Eastern and western history is full of such great *if's*.

The side of the Good also, in human affairs, is similarly represented by great individual reformers of religion, like Vyāsa and Buddha, Zoroaster and Moses, Christ and Muhammad, or beneficent monarchs like Ashoka the Priya-darshī (the "loving-eyed"), Marcus Aurelius the Stoic-Saint, and Nausherwãn the Just, or great merchant-benefactors of their peoples, the builders of great temples and "pious works" and endowers of long-lasting charities, Tirumala Rãya and Trilochana, Bimal Sãh and Bhãmã Sãh, Johns Hopkins and Leland Stanford, Carnegie and Rockefeller, etc..

In short, the individual "I" has been predominant. But only predominant; not all, not everything.

The " We," the col-lec-tion, the "together-binding", of individuals, has obviously never been altogether absent; otherwise the "I" would have disappeared too; but it has been greatly sub-dominant, sub- ordinate.

The Turn of Socialism

The Thread-Soul, the Over-soul, seems latterly to have become somewhat surfeited with this experience. It seem to want a change, it has perhaps had enough taste of the pungent sweets and corrosive acids of excessive individualism, in the persons of the individuals who constitute the cells and tissues of its vast earth-wide and aeonian body. It perhaps now wishes to taste the milder sweets and salts, the more moderate and wholesome astringents and appetising bitters, of Socialism, in and through the masses of its constituent members.

On the wide expanse of the plains of Thought, the plains of Philosophy, Science, Art, Religion, the idea of an Anima Mundi, a Vishv-ãtma, a Ruĥ-î-kul, a principle of Universal Consciousness, of a Common All- pervading life, of Unconscious Infinite and Eternal Ideation or Supra-conscious Will-and-Imagination, of an Oversoul of which all individual souls and bodies whatsoever are as the cells of a single organism, and which Oversoul, is, in its highest form, ultimately, none else than the eternally self-evident Self, A̍tmã, in and of all living beings, the Self-proven proof of all proofs; the idea of the Organic Unity and Continuity of Nature as the raiment of the one Supreme Spirit or Self; the idea of the consequent Brotherhood of Man; the idea of Physical Science and Art extending on all sides of their present limits into super-physical regions, explorable by means of subtler senses latent and evolvable in the human being — these ideas are dawning more and more brightly on the horizon of those plains (— though the advertisements, in the Western papers, especially those of the land of the Almighty Dollar, show that this growing harvest of "spirituality" is also being turned into cash diligently !). And the fresh Revelation, of consciously Scientific Religion, this time, seems likely to be made, not suddenly all at once and by a single individual as hitherto, but slowly and gradually by the large body of religious, scientific, and philosophical thinkers of the world working more or less deliberately in co-operation for the purpose.

In Politics, monarchism is being replaced by republicanism, autocracy by democracy (—though democracy, in the far as well as the middle West, continues to be hood-winked and wire-pulled almost worse than ever before by the vested, interests of plutocracy *cum* aristocracy *cum* theocracy, and, if released from this control, threatens to become "mobocracy"). National clawings and fangings are being attempted to be abated by an International League of Nations (— though that League does not include, does indeed deliberately exclude, in the spirit of the hypocrite and the bully combined, representatives of the bulk of mankind composed of the weaker exploitable and "mandate-"able peoples, so that even European observers have written of "the rapacious spirit ... of the mandatories"). It is much that the last vast surge of action, the Great War, has been interpreted as "a War to end War"(even though the snarlings and spittings continue as bad as ever almost). Thanks to the loss of flesh and blood, literal and metaphorical, there is at least wide-spread talk of a general disarmament, of shedding the fangs and claws (— even though, instead of the remnants of these being shed, the broken ones are being, or, rather, have already been, repaired and renewed, and the lost ones replaced, and, moreover, are being supplemented with stronger and fiercer beak and talon of aeroplane and shark's teeth of submarine). Even generals who took "distinguished" part in the Great Butchery are lecturing to the public on the *futility* of tooth-and-nail methods. And peace-movements and youth-movements are growing in many countries.

Russia has initiated, though in a setting of much violence, a tremendous experiment in a new form of political government expressly subservient to Economic Socialism, Karl Marx's *Das Capital* being reported to be the Soviet's Bible. But it seems to be already modifying the governing ideas thereof, as regards abolition of private property, considerably, so far as even Russians themselves are concerned, besides granting very long leases to foreign concessionaires and capitalist-profiteers, for developing the natural resources of the country, with entire exemption from the laws, as to limitation of property, which govern the Russians. And it is not at all possible yet to say how far the experiment will succeed. China is also engaged in a vast struggle with another experiment. Other countries, in the near West, Turkey, Afghanistan, Arabia, Egypt, are all heaving with new ideas of Government.

More important to Indians than all these, and of greater promise for the well-being of humanity, is the bringing into the field of politics, by Mahãtmã Gãndhĩ, for the helping of the exploited weaker peoples, and amongst them too of the vast poorer masses especially, as their best weapon, of the method of passive resistance to, civil disobedience of, "non-violent non-co-operation" with, evil generally and all evil Government specially. This new application of the principle and policy of the ancient *hartãl* and *tyãga* of India (expressive of public disapproval and dissent generally, on all sorts of occasions, but mostly with reference to unpopular administrative measures of the ruler of the day), and of the modern Western economic "general strike", to the sphere of politics, is a true inspiration given to Mahātmā Gandhî by the Oversoul of Humanity for reducing the horrors of war, and will, bye and bye, let us fervently hope, justify the anciently recognised fact, *Ex Oriente Lux*, in Politics as in Religion and Philosophy. It is a noble endeavour to demonstrate *practically* and on an immense scale in politics, the philosophical and ethical truth that hatred can be conquered more successfully by (intelligently and passively resistant, and not merely submissive and acquiescent) love than by hatred.

Such are the signs of the new activity of the Oversoul, in Politics.

In the domain of Economics also, the idea of co-operation is growing into greater and greater prominence and importance, co-operation between producers, between them and capitalists, between both and consumers; the idea that co-operation, "mutual alliance". is more necessary for the progress, the life, the very existence of the race than competition and struggle (as excellently expounded in Prince Kropotkin's *Mutual Aid*, almost the first scientific counter-blast to and corrective of the extreme elements in the Darwinian "mutual struggle").

That Socialism can run into as great extremes (wherein lies error, invariably) as Individualism, is indicated, in the department of War, by the completeness with which so many nations were organised (in the way of compulsive autocratic despotic state-socialism) for the Great War, as they have never yet been organised for peace; and, in the department of Domesticity, by the practical promiscuity which is reported to be under experiment in Russia, on the avowed ground (as explained, *e.g.,* by Mme. Kollontoi, a Russian official) that "the communist society has no use for the old form of the family"... the bourgeois monogamy"... which is "destructively individualistic in its influence", and clashes with "socialist ideals"; that, "in short, the narrowing, selfish, clannish emotions of the family-life" should be expanded to communal dimensions. The great danger of state-socialism is that, with the very best of intentions, it may become the very acme, the *reductio ad absurdum et horrendum*, of individualism, of Bureaucracy, of the enslavement and mechanisation of the vast majority by a handful of individuals.

Different Aspects of Individualism and Socialism

We thus see that in all departments of human life, new ideas, new feelings, new enterprises, which are the reverse of those that have so far held sway, are slowly, with many backslidings, many a slip 'twixt the cup and the lip', slowly forcing themselves into prominence in human affairs.

In terms of Psychology, the mass-mind rather than the single particular mind; of History, the people rather than the king and the hero; of Ethics, altruism rather than egoism; of Science, Unconscious or Supra-conscious Spiritualism rather than materialism; of Religion, Spiritual Rationalism and Universal Brotherhood rather than unquestioning faith, blind *credo*, sectarianism and shibboleths; in Politics, internationalism or humanism rather than nationalism, and democracy rather than autocracy; in Economics, regulated co-operation rather than free competition, society rather than the individual. All these pairs of opposites are inseparably allied aspects of the same ultimate, or rather, penultimate metaphysical pair, the One Spirit and the Many Matter; and, therefore the sufficient prevailing of any member of any pair over its opposite will be sooner or later followed by the prevailing of all its corresponding members in all the pairs over their respective opposites.

The Most Important Aspect

For our present purposes, the pair of Socialism and Individualism is the most important. The Dawn of "Another Renaissance", hoped for by large numbers of human beings in all countries today, depends upon the achievement of successful domination, by a *just* and *rational* (and not extremist) Socialism (we will not say "spiritual" socialism lest some worthy readers be repelled), over the now unrestrained Individualism.

That all fundamental human problems have to be threshed out today primarily in the economic terms of Individualism and Socialism, is evidenced by the fact of the ever-growing literature upon the subject of the antagonism between these two; by the many varieties into which Socialism has become sub-divided, each advocated by an important and influential school of thinkers; by the frequency with which the terms meet the eye in ephemeral but influential journalism as well as in somewhat more lasting but less wide-reaching books, even when other subjects are being directly dealt with; by the fact that all the newer textbooks, professedly and expressly, of "political science", make sure to give large and prominent place to a discussion of this pair; by such a violently striking fact as that above referred to, of the *political* revolution of Russia being based on the *economic* ideas of Socialism; and, more than all else, by the simple, unmistakable, unquestionable fact that political institutions have no other just and rational aim than to subserve the *economic* needs of the people, in the larger sense of the word, from the Greek *oikos*, and the Samskrt *okas*, meaning the house, the home. States originate, and are developed, governments exist, and are maintained by the people, in order that "homes" may be happy, through the securing and the assuring (*yoga* and *kshema*) to the people, by the State and the Government, of all the requirements of the happy home; they have no other *raison d'être*.

The Close-Knit Web of Human Life

Now "homes" cannot be happy without an "equitable distribution", to all families, of the *physical*, as well as the *psychical* means of happiness, *artha* in Samskrt (*i.e.*, in the broader view, the four *purush-ārthas*, aims or ends of human life); for "men do not live by bread alone"; they want *panem et circenses*; and the *circenses* take different forms for different temperaments.

Such equitable distribution is not possible without a fairly complete, comprehensively thought out, balanced "social organisation", in Samskrt, *samājavyasthā*. Opportunist, haphazard, temporising patch- work might possibly palliate for a while, but will, like most quack remedies, ultimately aggravate the disease. When it is so serious as to have affected all the organs, nothing less than a complete overhauling, and constitutional treatment by alternatives, will do.

Social organisation means "division of labour", *karma-vibhāga*.

Successful and efficient division of labour is possible only when there is a scientifically correct "classification of psycho-physical temperaments" (idiosyncrasies, inclinations, dispositions, special abilities, vocational aptitudes, etc.), and all individuals are grouped into a few main "classes" corresponding with the main temperaments (the man of knowledge, the man of action, the man of acquisitive desire, all differentiating and specialising, by "spontaneous variation", out of the unskilled or little-skilled workman as the general plasm); *i.e.*, when there is *varna-vyavasthā* or *chātur-varnya*, not hereditary but temperamental.

Such classification is possible only when the "educational system" is properly organised, and the aptitude ascertained, by appropriate methods, during the "school-and-college" days, of each individual pupil; the *guru-kula* system.

The grouping of the people into vocational classes, and the division of the social labour between these classes, fulfil their purpose only when appropriate functions or vocations with appurtenant appropriate rights and duties, are assigned to persons of corresponding psycho-physical temperaments; *dharma- karma-vibhāga.*

In order that the persons to whom the functions are assigned may discharge them adequately, means of subsistence must be assured to them. For this there must be a corresponding division of "means of livelihood", leading, as a consequence, to an equitable division of "the necessaries of life", and the securing of a minimum-comfort living to all; *vrtti-vibhāga* or *jivikā-vibhāga*. Such division of the means of livelihood between the several classes, the insistence that each order or class shall gain its living by pursuit of only such bread-winning or money, making avocations as are fixed for it, will regulate and restrain the play of the individualistic instinct, and will prevent the blind and frantic competition wherein each and every individual is permitted by the *laissez faire* policy, to grab at all kinds of "livelihood", *i.e.*, money-making methods, at one and the same time. "Necessaries of life", it may be noted here, ordinarily mean the objects of the "physical" appetites, food .and clothing, spouse, dwelling- place, and subsidiaries.

"Efficient and whole-hearted performance of appropriate function" by each individual is possible, further, only when a corresponding division is made of the "luxuries of life", the rewards and prizes of life. For, as said before, men do not live by bread alone, and they need other things for their *psychical* satisfaction, which things, incidentally, act as "individualistic" *incentives* to them to put forth the best that is in them, in their respective vocations. The "luxuries of life" *toshanā-s rādhasa-s, ārādhana-s* are the objects of the "psychical" appetites or ambitions, *eshanā's*. These are, mainly, *honor, power, wealth,* and *amusement*, corresponding to the four main temperament's. This partition of the main ambitions and satisfactions would, in Samskrt, be called, *éshanā-toshanā-vibhāga*.

In order that all this may be done, all these divisions and partitions made and worked, it is necessary that there should be, firstly, wise "legislation", providing for them, and, secondly, firm "execution", giving actual effect to the provisions of the law. Finally, in order that there may be such legislation and execution, the people, whose "homes" are to be made happy, must "select and elect" from among themselves, their *best* and *wisest*, their *most philanthropic* and *most capable*, in short, the *higher self* of the community, to be the legislators and directors of the executive.

So is the "virtuous circle" completed. So are all departments of human life, educational, political, economic, domestic, all "organs" of the social organism, closely and inseparably connected together, educative-legislative head, executive-regulative arm, sustentative - distributive trunk, all-supporting - industrial legs — all vitalised by the heart, *viz.*, the "home". [For fuller exposition of these and the following ideas, see the author's *The Science of Social Organization,* or *The Laws of Manu in the Light of Theosophy*]

Psychical Causes and Effects

The genuinely "communistic" organisations of the communities of early Christian monks, dwelling in very large numbers in the monasteries of the Egyptian Thebaid, with every circumstance favourable for success, yet split on this rock, *viz.*, the lack of the impetus to work, the incentives, the spurs to activity, of the *toshanā-s*, the objects of the various ambitions, above mentioned. As Gibbon says, in describing their attempts and their failure (in ch. xxvii of his great work on *The Roman Empire*): "The industry must be faint and languid which is not excited by the sense of *personal interest*." The practical experiments of Robert Owen and of other communists of the U.S.A. [*Vide* Leacock, *Elements of Political Science,* chapter "Socialism"] who have tried, in America, to establish socialist colonies, have split on the same rock. Many plans, regarding the abolition of all private property, of the Russian Bolshevik Soviet Government, are reported to have been upset by the same difficulty. Example of another kind of trouble, also psychical, is the case of experiments also tried in the West, especially the U.S.A., on the lines of a suggestion of J. S. Mill's, *viz.*, workmen's unions buying up and managing factories. The managing officers, who have had to be appointed unavoidably, have, before long, developed the bureaucratic and autocratic spirit. But why need we go to these distant examples ? Why not go to the very familiar and close at hand archetype itself of all socialism and communism, the joint family of India? There, if anywhere, should the socialist maxim work, and does work to whatever extent it does so at all, the maxim, *viz.*, "From each according to his capacity and to each according to his needs". The maxim governs the joint family only so long as a common ancestor remains alive. He or she is the human embodiment of the maxim, and also of a benevolent and righteous "state-force" which *un- selfishly, lovingly, impartially, and therefore unresistedly*, compels all the members of the family to observe it in their conduct. As soon as that strong thread breaks, the beads scatter apart. For selfishness, laziness, jealousies, in short, evil motives, gain the upper hand, which formerly had been kept under by the good motives felt and spread and imposed by the common ancestor. The socialist maxim suffers, in the hands of most workers, whether with brain or with muscle, "a great change, into something very strange" and very familiar, *viz.*, "The least that I must do and the most that I can take". In the hands of the "mighty", it undergoes the Roman variation: "

From all the provinces according to their utmost capacity, and to Rome according to the needs of its wildest and most luxurious caprice and avarice". This is the guiding maxim of the governments seated in the huge capital-towns of the advanced nations of the West, today, especially those "owning" "dependencies" (whose inhabitants cannot become emperors, as Roman provincials could) — the capital towns "which waste in each night's bout the wealth of kings". The new somewhat conventional "central authority". the "managing director" as distinguished from the deceased natural head, of the family, not inspired by the same love of all the youngers, and not inspiring the same confidence and respect, consciously or unconsciously begins to absorb the bulk of the property, the earnings, the advantages. Or the junior members shirk work but want to share profits and share alike. Or each mother tries to secure extra comforts for her children. Bickerings begin. The joint family breaks up into a number of separate families. The process is repeated generation after generation.

Socialist-politicians have this patent psychological fact before their eyes, obtrusively. Yet the many schemes and books put forth by the various schools of socialism do not touch it, much less grapple with it, in its *psychical aspect*. There is perhaps a rare exception here and there. Thus the "conscientious objector" of the war-days, mathematician, sociologist, and philosopher, Mr. Bertrand Russell recognises (in his book, *Roads to Freedom*) that the causes of human troubles are *psychological*. He seems also to have caught the old Indian idea of duly utilising, and regulating, honor, power, and wealth as incentives, but has touched the subject very cursorily. Some writers of systematic text-books on Political Science also recognise that "Socialists are inclined to be too optimistic in underrating the psychological obstacles to their plan". The brilliant Mr. G. B. Shaw, in his *Guide to Socialism* (pub. 1928), while exceedingly lucid in most of his chapters, is equally unsatisfactory and completely unconvincing in his treatment of the " Incentive" to work and of "the will to equality" which he recognises to be the main desideratum, but for the creation of which, in any given nation or society, not to speak of mankind at large, he can. suggest no means.

The difficulty is indeed a psychical one. Therefore psychical remedies, working by internal stimulation, automatically and perpetually from within each individual concerned — and all individuals are concerned — are needed. Devices, more or less mechanical, operating from outside, by external compulsion alone, are bound to fail. Compulsion from outside must be helped, if it cannot be wholly supplanted, by impulsion from within. If reports be true, in Bolshevik Russia peasants began to avoid producing more than was "necessary of life" for themselves more than they were allowed by the Soviet State to keep. Why should they produce more, for the State to take away, for alleged purposes which did not come home to them at all, in their daily life ? They saw no fun in doing so. They had not the necessary "patriotism". Even "patriotism" requires *aliment*. That nourishment is psychical — honor, power, wealth, amusement. Let it be noted here that, while the joys of honor and power are obviously psychical, wealth too does not mean mere collections of securities, notes, coins or other physical objects as such, but the *joy* of artistic possessions and of helping (or in the case of the evil-minded, hindering) others. Manu, the oldest law-giver cf the oldest living civilisation of the earth (except perhaps the Chinese) and his compatriot philosophers, have left behind the needed guidance on this point, as to how the natural psychical appetites, the *eshanā-s*, the ambitions, of the different types of temperament, and their respective objects, *toshanā-s*, honor, etc., should be utilised as incentives to effort, as competitive, *individualistic*, motives to excel in *socialistic public spirit* and *public service*, for the organisation of the Society of the Human Race, and the due performance of the social labour. It is only when the sovereign-body, the central authority, the selected and elected (honorary, unsalaried) Legislature (and Director and Supervisor of the Executive) in a State, approximates, *ethically* as well as intellectually, in largeness of heart as well as ripeness of experienced wisdom, to the living patriarch of the joint family, that the longed- for reconciliation between Individualism and Socialism will be approximated to in that state. And this is not impossible if high ethical and intellectual qualifications are prescribed for "electees", and if electors are systematically educated to wisely choose persons possessing those qualifications and so approximating to the Higher Self of the "nation", or better, the "people", of the State. As a recent American writer says: [Ford, *Representative Government,* pub. 1925] "How to reconcile representative institutions", *i.e.,* self-government, "with good government has become the great problem of the day". *This problem will be solved only when it is widely recognised that self-government means government by the higher, and not the lower, Self of the people, legislation by representatives who are ethically as well as intellectually worthy, who are disinterested and philanthropic as well as possessed of mature experience, special knowledge, sound judgment.* This recognition of the Higher Self is the very quintessential secret of the solution of all the problems of Padagogics, Domestics, Economics, Civics, Politics, Ethics, Philosophy, Religion, Spirituality, all at once. In every department of human life in which human embodiments and exponents of this *higher* Self are allowed to guide the conduct of affairs — in every such department success and happiness will result. And such wide recognition is not impossible to achieve, if systematic teaching and preaching is carried on through press and platform, by even a few convinced and resolute persons to begin with, to expound the fairly obvious fact that legislators must be good and wise if laws are to be good and wise, and to explain what are "the outward symbols of the inward grace", the marks whereby the worthiness of the persons to be elected may be recognised, and the means by which they may be persuaded to shoulder the burden of the legislator's duty (instead of hustling and struggling, bribing and flattering and begging shamelessly, and intimidating and bullying, to secure votes). Then (as Mr. G. B. Shaw also recognises, at last, near the end of his large book) will self-government be justified of its name, and Individualism and Socialism be reconciled, and the Renaissance come.

www.ingramcontent.com/pod-product-compliance
Lightning Source LLC
LaVergne TN
LVHW041501070426
835507LV00009B/742